THE
CAT WHO
THINKS
SHE IS A PIG

And Other Stories
We Write Together

ONCE UPON A PANCAKE
Making Reading and Writing Fun

THE CAT WHO THINKS SHE IS A PIG

And Other Stories We Write Together

STARTED BY RICK BENGER

Collins

An imprint of HarperCollins*PublishersLtd*

WRITTEN BY

THAT'S YOU!
WRITE YOUR NAMES

STARTED BY Rick Benger

LEAD ILLUSTRATION BY Maddie Egremont

EDITED BY Karin Fisher-Golton

COVER DESIGN BY Zeena Baybayan

A NOTE FOR GROWN-UPS

This book is suitable for children ages 3–5 (or so), who typically can't yet read or write. You'll help by reading the stories out loud and writing down the children's ideas. It's best to transcribe word-for-word, so they can fully experience the power of their own storytelling. Don't worry about tying the stories up with beginnings, middles, and ends—the joy is in setting the imagination free and capturing creativity on the page.

The real magic begins when you take turns to imagine what happens next. It helps to use a different color for each storyteller, e.g. red for Maria, green for Harry, blue for Mom.

HAVE FUN!
RICK

P.S. For finished story examples and other creative inspiration, take a peek at our Instagram (@uponapancake) and website (onceuponapancake.com).

Tommy's hair will not do what it is told.

He tries to fix it with his hands, but it won't stay in place.

He tries to fix it with a brush, but it *still* won't stay in place.

He tries to fix it with a comb, but that makes it even worse!

So he tries to fix it with

DRAW
TOMMY'S
STUBBORN
HAIR

STORY #1

WHAT DOES
TOMMY'S HAIR
LOOK LIKE
AFTERWARD?
DRAW IT!

STORY #1

Sydney likes all four seasons.
   She likes summer because

....

....

....

....

   She likes spring because

....

....

....

....

   She likes winter because

....

....

....

....

   But fall is her favorite season because

....

....

....

....

WHAT DOES SYDNEY DO IN FALL?

L auren has a cat that thinks she is a pig.

"OINK!" says the cat.

Lauren also has a dog.

The dog thinks he is a ....

....

....

....

....

WHAT DOES THE DOG SAY?

OINK!

One day, Lauren's cat and dog ....

....

....

....

....

....

....

....

....

....

....

....

....

....

....

....

....

....

← WHO? ADD A NAME

.... has found a key in the garden.

A big key.

A big, fancy key.

A big, fancy, golden key!

DRAW THE BIG, ↗
FANCY, GOLDEN KEY

.... picks up the key, and
it starts to glow. And then ....

....

....

DOES THE KEY
OPEN SOMETHING?

STORY #4

Anna is walking by the barn.

She hears "cluck-cluck-cluck-cluck-cluck." That is the

....

She hears "moooooooo." That is the

....

She hears "baaaaaaaa." That is the

....

Then Anna hears a very surprising sound. She hears

"

....

WHAT ELSE IS
IN THE BARN?

....

....

....

.... KEEP GOING . . .

....

DRAW IT! ↘

STORY #5

. . . CONTINUED

THEN WHAT
HAPPENS IN
THE BARN?

STORY #5

STORY #5

Jennifer and her family live by the train tracks. Jennifer loves to watch the trains go by.

One afternoon a special train comes along. The cars are all different colors, and bubbles are coming out of the engine's smokestack!

STORY #6

WHAT HAPPENS
WHEN THE
SPECIAL TRAIN
GOES BY?

STORY #6

Brandon has a peculiar pet.

His pet is a cloud.

The cloud just showed up one day, above his head. Now everywhere Brandon goes, the cloud goes too.

WHAT DO BRANDON
AND HIS CLOUD
DO TOGETHER?

STORY #7

STORY #7

Sophia gets to be a dinosaur for one day.
        She chooses to be a ....

....

because ....

....

and ....

....

WHAT TYPE OF DINOSAUR DOES SOPHIA CHOOSE?

WHERE DOES SHE GO?

....

....

....

....

....

....

....

....

DRAW SOPHIA
THE DINOSAUR

KEEP GOING . . .

STORY #8

...CONTINUED

WHO DOES SOPHIA
THE DINOSAUR MEET?

STORY #8

R iley the fox has a super-smelling nose.

He can smell exactly when the bakery in town has finished its first batch of bread.

He can smell when it's going to rain, hours before the first raindrop falls.

He can even smell ....

....

....

....

One morning, Riley smells ....

....

....

....

....

....

....

....

....

WHAT DOES RILEY DO ABOUT THE SMELL?

STORY #10

Princess .... lives in a
castle in the sky.

....

....

....

WHO ELSE
LIVES THERE?

....

....

....

....

....

....

....

....

KEEP GOING . . .

STORY #10

... CONTINUED

WHAT
HAPPENS
INSIDE THE
CASTLE?

DRAW THE
PRINCESS!

Jonas's favorite toy is missing.

Jonas is worried. He feels funny in his tummy. Where could his toy be?

He looks inside. He looks outside. He can't find it anywhere.

So his mom helps him make some posters, which they put up in their neighborhood.

DRAW JONAS'S TOY

MISSING!

STORY #11

WHAT DID JONAS
DO NEXT?

DID JONAS
FIND HIS TOY?

Kiara loves her white dress.

She would like to wear it every day. But she can't wear it every day, because it never stays white for long. It becomes a many-colored messy dress and needs to go in the wash.

This morning, her dress is already a little bit green because

WHAT OTHER
MESSES DOES
KIARA GET ON
HER DRESS?

COLOR KIARA'S
MANY-COLORED
MESSY DRESS!

STORY #12

M ia is at the aquarium. She is trying to count the fish. How many are there? It's hard to tell! They keep swimming away.

Finally, she has counted them all. There are .... fish. And she has counted much more than fish.

In fact, there are:

.... jellyfish

.... crabs

.... stingrays

.... sharks

STORY #13

And could it be? One mermaid!

WHAT HAPPENS
NEXT?

KEEP GOING . . .

STORY #13

. . . CONTINUED

DRAW! ☺

STORY #13

L ily and Ravi made their best fort ever.
They made it out of ....

....

and ....

and ....

....

....

DRAW THE
FORT!
←

STORY #14

Now the fort is done. Lily and Ravi crawl inside, and

Eli the elephant helps at the fire department.
He's too big to fit inside the fire truck. The firefighters attach a special trailer to the back, so Eli can ride along.

OH NO! WHAT'S ON FIRE?

STORY #15

DRAW ELI
ON HIS
SPECIAL
TRAILER

↙

KEEP GOING . . .

. . . CONTINUED

HOW DOES
ELI HELP?

STORY #15

Noah starts to draw a horse.

But the horse begins to look more like a dragon! So he decides to turn it into a dragon.

Then it starts to look like ....

So he turns it into ....

....

....

....

....

....

....

....

WHAT HAPPENS
WHEN NOAH FINISHES
HIS DRAWING?

....

....

....

....

STORY #16

RECREATE NOAH'S DRAWING!

(YOU COULD TAKE TURNS, ONE PERSON
STARTING WITH A HORSE)

Owen and Paola are fighting about zebras.

Owen says they are white with black stripes.

Paola says they are black with white stripes.

"I'm right!" says Owen.

"No, I'm right!" says Paola.

They fight and fight until Owen says, "I don't know anymore. White or black? Black or white? How do we know who's right?"

"I know!" says Paola. "We should ask a zebra."

WHERE DO
THEY FIND A
ZEBRA TO ASK?

STORY #17

STORY #17

STORY #18

Claudio loves the Moon.

  He knows many facts about it.

He knows it is more than 200,000 miles from Earth.

He knows the Sun shines on it, and that's why it glows.

And he knows ....

....

....

He loves to watch it most when ....

....

....

....

....

WHAT HAPPENS WHEN
CLAUDIO WATCHES
THE MOON?

....

....

....

....

....

....

KEEP GOING . . .

....

STORY #18

...CONTINUED

One night, when the Moon is especially bright and beautiful, Claudio

STORY #18

O scar the crab lives in a shiny shell at the bottom of the deep blue sea.

Oscar is sad because he has found a hole in his shell.

COLOR
OSCAR IN!

"Oh no!" says Oscar. "How can I fix my shell? Maybe if

I sing a song, I'll feel better and figure out what to do."

So Oscar sings:

Oh dear, there's a hole. Oh no! Oh dear!

A hole in my shell, oh dear! Oh no!

FINISH
HIS
SONG

WHAT DOES
OSCAR DO ABOUT
HIS SHELL?

STORY #19

NEW STORY!
HOW DOES IT BEGIN?

....
....
....
....

WHOA!
WHO ARE
THEY?

STORY #20

WHO DO THEY HELP?

STORY #20

George and his friend ....
are walking through the woods, on the way to ....
.... ,

when George sees a little log cabin.

George stops and says to his friend, " ....
....
....
....
....

WHAT DOES GEORGE DO NEXT?

This is Milly the ice cream truck.

Milly has a little problem—she's run out of all her normal ice cream flavors!

She has no more ....

And no more ....

And only the teeniest tiniest scoop of ....

....

So Milly decides to try something new.

....

WHAT DOES MILLY TRY?

COLOR HER IN! ↓

DOES MILLY GO
ANYWHERE?
DOES SHE MEET
ANYBODY?

....

....

....   WHAT HAPPENS
                                                                                                         IN THE END?
....

....

....

                                                                ....

        DRAW
     WHATEVER ☺   ....
      YOU LIKE!

              ↓

STORY #22

HarperCollins books may be purchased for educational, business,
or sales promotional use through our Special Markets Department.

HarperCollins Publishers Ltd
Bay Adelaide Centre, East Tower
22 Adelaide Street West, 41st Floor
Toronto, Ontario, Canada
M5H 4E3

www.harpercollins.ca

ISBN 978-1-4434-7099-5

Printed and bound in Latvia
PNB 9 8 7 6 5 4 3 2 1

RICK BENGER is the creator of Once upon a Pancake, a series of interactive books with unfinished stories inside. He occasionally writes stories all by himself—a selection of which can be found at rickbenger.com, where you'll also find his newsletter about being a new dad.